Original title:
Salt on the Breeze

Author: Derek Caldwell

ISBN HARDBACK: 978-1-80581-668-3
ISBN PAPERBACK: 978-1-80581-195-4
ISBN EBOOK: 978-1-80581-668-3

Saline Secrets on the Wind

Waves giggle as they splash,
Seagulls steal fries in a dash.
Shells whisper tales of the sea,
While crabs dance in jubilee.

Laughter rides on the tide,
Fish swim with silly pride.
The sun grins, the sky's a tease,
Life's a joke, so just seize.

Tides Carrying Memory's Echo

The ocean sings of things once lost,
A flip-flop here, a drink's cost.
Funny how the past can float,
Like seaweed caught on a coat.

Old beach towels tell their tales,
As friends recount their epic fails.
The surf hums a silly tune,
While daydreams scatter like balloons.

An Ode to the Nautical Wind

Oh, breeze, you tease with your dance,
You tousle my hair, give me a chance!
You whisper jokes that only you know,
Tickling my toes as you blow.

With each gust, a laugh unfolds,
Sweaters and hats fly, the fun beholds.
Chasing kites up in the air,
I trip and laugh without a care.

Mist and Spray in Evening Light

Evening mist brings a shivery grin,
As fish joke about whose turn to win.
The tide rolls in with a cheeky clap,
Waves hula-hoop, now that's no trap!

Sunset colors the splashy game,
A jellyfish floats, but it's not the same.
Memories dance in the murky hue,
As laughter and ocean collide anew.

Cradled by the Ocean’s Breath

A crab rolled by, wearing a grin,
His little legs tapping, he’d surely win.
Seagulls are squawking, making a scene,
While fish are practicing to be on screen.

The waves are laughing, oh what a jest,
A mermaid's wig floats down, she’s not impressed.
Shells gossip and giggle in the sun's warm glow,
While seaweed dances, stealing the show.

Secrets Carried by Hopeful Winds.

There's a dolphin who dreams, sings songs of delight,
But his voice sounds more like a cat in a plight.
Wind whispers sweet nothings to the tall pines,
While crabs throw parties, serving up brine.

A bid to the gulls, "Hey, come grab a seat!"
They laugh and they squawk, then steal all the treats.
In this ocean ballet, where chaos reigns,
The fish roll their eyes, but what fun it gains!

Whispers of the Tidal Muse

The tide comes in, bringing a joke,
But the sandcastles fear, they might just choke.
A starfish recites his funny old rhyme,
While octopuses clap, they've run out of time.

The shells keep on squeaking, they’re tickled pink,
As the tide’s playful fingers start to wink.
Flotsam and jetsam begin their charade,
Laughter echoes as shadows invade.

Ocean's Breath at Dusk

As the sun dips low, the colors collide,
A crab with a bowtie is on quite a ride.
The wind stirs up mischief, tossing the hats,
While the ocean chuckles, chatting with cats.

The twilight finds mermaids having a ball,
Splashing and giggling, away goes the wall.
With moonlight chuckling, the tales start to soar,
As fish put on shows, we beg them for more.

Gentle Whispers from the Horizon

Seagulls squawk with tales to tell,
Their jokes are bad, but we laugh so well.
Waves keep rolling like a silly tide,
As crabs do the cha-cha, there's nowhere to hide.

Shells are scattered, a treasure chest,
The sand's a blanket, we take a rest.
A dolphin pops up with a cheeky grin,
He's playing peek-a-boo, let the fun begin!

Weathered boats bob in a comical dance,
Each wave's a partner in a goofy romance.
A pirate's hat flops on a hapless head,
As we giggle at tales that the ocean has read.

So let's sip lemonade, under palm tree sway,
Chasing away the worries of the day.
With laughter ringing like a joyful tune,
We'll dance like the sea, beneath the moon!

Nautical Dreams in Swayed Sweetness

On a sandy shore where the flip-flops lie,
We dive for joy like fish that fly.
A crab holds court with a waving pincher,
While seaweed's tangled like a wild adventure.

The beach ball bounces, oh what a sight,
It hits a seagull, and takes a flight.
Sandcastles crumble, with kings in despair,
As tourists build moats that just aren't fair!

We trade our worries for shells and sand,
Making goofy masks with a silly hand.
With windswept hair and bright, loud shirts,
We laugh at our sunburns and silly flirts.

So let's raise our cups to a day well spent,
With squinty eyes and laughter's scent.
Under the sun with our joyful crew,
We find the humor in every view!

Tranquil Thoughts on Ocean's Breath

Waves are chuckling with a playful glee,
As fish make faces, just wait and see.
A starfish grins from his rock parade,
While our laughter swirls like a silly braid.

Tide pools bubble like laughing pots,
With little crabs playing lots of slots.
Octopus jugglers in a slippery show,
While clams play music, just go with the flow!

A beach tent flaps like an overexcited dog,
As kids build dreams in a sandy fog.
Flip-flops forgotten, the chase begins,
As we zoom down the shore like ocean twins.

So here we are, with sunshine bright,
Finding the humor in each delight.
With every giggle, we weave our song,
In the seaside laughter, we all belong!

Currents of Memory in the Foam

The waves bring tales from days gone by,
Of goofy swims and sandcastles high.
Seagulls squawk with a comedic flair,
While sunscreen slips through careless hair.

A crab in a bowtie makes a grand show,
Dancing on shells, putting on a slow glow.
The tide pulls back with a giggling sound,
As we chase memories, laughter all around.

Drifting with the Sea's Embrace

Floating along with a silly grin,
As jellyfish dance and the sea stars spin.
A fish in a tutu sways with delight,
While seaweed tickles, oh what a sight!

We spot a message in a bottle, you see,
It’s a cocktail recipe signed by a bee.
The ocean’s humor leaves us amused,
With every splash, feeling so bemused.

A Caress of Coastal Essence

The shore writes stories in grains of sand,
With footprints dancing, so unplanned.
A whale in a hat takes a bow on its tail,
As laughter bubbles up with each tale.

A starfish winks from its spot on the rock,
Claiming it's fashion, so round with a shock.
We gather these moments, a treasure in glee,
As the waves giggle softly, just you and me.

Salty Hues of Dusk's Palette

At twilight’s fringe the colors collide,
As seagulls and crabs join the fun-filled ride.
The sun dips low, it’s a clown with a hat,
Painting the sky in shades of chitchat.

Pineapple drinks spill over the ledge,
A beach ball bounces from the water’s edge.
As shadows grow long and laughter unfurls,
The night wraps us tight in its sparkling swirls.

A Chorus for the Free-Flowing Seas

When the waves start to giggle, and fish play a tune,
You know it's a party, beneath the full moon.
Crabs dance along, with a swaggering stride,
As seagulls join in, on this wild ocean ride.

All the seaweed sways to the rhythm of fun,
Jellyfish jiggle, they're all on the run.
Fishermen laugh as they try to compete,
But the octopus winks, saying, "You can't take my beat!"

A dolphin will leap with a splash and a grin,
While the clam shells come out for the dance to begin.
Life's a vast ocean, where chaos can reign,
But in this big party, it's all joy, no pain.

So raise your sea glass, let the laughter resound,
For every small wave holds a joke to be found.
When sailors go fishing for tales that amuse,
They'll find every wave is a laughter-fueled muse.

Tales Carried by the Whispering Gales

The clouds tell stories, drifting so high,
Of mischievous kites that just want to fly.
With laughter they bounce, like leaves in a whirl,
As the breeze carries tales, a joyful swirl.

Sailboats are skimming, with sails like big grins,
Their captains all joking, where mischief begins.
A crab in a top hat, a fish with a tie,
Plotting their antics, oh my, oh my!

Cockleshell jokes echo across sunny bays,
As gulls crack wise with their silly displays.
The wind, like a bard, with a sly little tease,
Delivers the tales of our frolicking seas.

So harness the gales, and let laughter fly,
For every good breeze brings a laugh, oh my!
The sea may be salty, but humor can thrive,
With tales from the winds, oh how we thrive!

Wildflower Currents in the Maritime Flow

In a field of wildflowers by the shore so grand,
The bees buzz around like they're in a band.
Petals wear colors like a clown's funny face,
As they dance by the currents with whimsical grace.

A curious raccoon with a wink and a grin,
Sips sweet nectar, thinking he's found a new kin.
Seagulls applaud with floppy foot flair,
While the sun starts to giggle, casting light everywhere.

The tide comes tumbling, bringing seashells galore,
Each one with a tale of a wave's clumsy chore.
Who knew the horizon hid jokes in its wave,
As wildflowers chuckle, the ocean they brave?

Join in on the laughter, both high and low,
In the merry marigold patch where the wildflowers grow.
For every bloom whispers secrets untold,
Of fun in the currents where sweet joy unfolds.

The Breeze that Guides Wayward Souls

In the twilight's glow, where the sand meets the sea,
A breeze tells a joke that makes everyone glee.
With a nudge on the surfers, it shouts, "Catch a ride!"
While the dolphins all snicker, oh what a pride!

An old sailor's yarn floats along on the air,
About a ghost ship sailing with matching footwear.
Mermaids join in, with their shimmering tails,
Singing sea shanties that jingle like gales.

Kites dance like children, zipping up high,
While the breeze pulls at pants with a playful cry.
Each gust brings a smile, as it twirls and it sways,
Guiding lost little boats through the comical haze.

So let the wayward wander where the dragons might sail,
For every light breeze carries a joke in its trail.
As laughter ignites on this whimsical coast,
We'll cheer for the wind, our ever-fun host!

Silken Clouds on the Open Water

Silken clouds dance in the sun,
Bobbing boats are having fun.
Seagulls dive for a tasty treat,
While waves play peekaboo with feet.

Catch a crab, his sideways glance,
He slips away, but what a dance!
With every splash, the laughter grows,
The ocean whispers all it knows.

Salt-Kissed Promises of Tomorrow

Breezy tales of woe and cheer,
Shells giggle as they draw near.
The ocean’s churn, a giant ride,
Watch your hat, it's full of pride!

Fish are grinning, scales on show,
They mock the surfers down below.
A dolphin waves, what a delight,
While sunburns form, oh what a sight!

Gentle Caress of the Waterfront

Waves are tickling sandy toes,
A child squeals as a seagull goes.
Sandcastles rise with lofty dreams,
But watch out! The tide has schemes!

Laughter rings, oh what a blast,
A wayward beachball flies too fast.
Fingers sticky, snacks galore,
Who knew folly could taste like more?

Ansel's Byway of the Riven Waves

Ansel calls, 'Let’s ride the tide!',
With goofy grins, we cannot hide.
Riven waves with splashes bright,
Bouncing in, oh what a sight!

Jellyfish giggle as they float,
While sandy critters make their note.
With a wink and a splash, we flee,
Adventure calls, come dance with me!

Wind-Worn Whispers of the Shore

The gulls conspire in flight,
Hatching plans that feel quite light.
They squawk and sway, oh what a show,
As if the sea is their own stage, you know.

Their feathers ruffled, sandy feet,
With snacks from the beach, they find a treat.
The wind's a clown, with tricks to share,
Poking fun at folks too busy to care.

With every wave a new surprise,
The tides tease us with playful lies.
Who knew the ocean's a mischievous mime,
Performing gags, one wave at a time?

As crabs dance sideways, quite a sight,
They scuttle about, giving us a fright.
Caught in laughter, the shoreline plays,
A comedy show beneath sun's rays.

The Sea's Embrace upon My Skin

The sunbeams tickle, oh so spry,
My toes in water, I let out a sigh.
The sea brushes gently, a silly kiss,
Who knew that nature could be like this?

A wave crashes loudly, splashing my face,
I yelp and giggle, what a wild race!
The ocean’s a prankster, a bubbly tease,
Wrestling with currents, blowing with ease.

My hat flies off, a lone seagull snags,
As I chase him down, I'm wearing rags.
Drenched in laughter, my hair's a mess,
Yet somehow I feel like I’m dressed to impress.

With each rise and fall, my spirits soar,
Nature's comedy, who could ask for more?
So here I frolic, as the sun settles in,
In this playful embrace, I’m sure to grin.

Lullabies of the Ocean's Edge

The waves hum softly, a sea-bound tune,
Swaying me gently under the moon.
Shells are my pillows, sand is my bed,
Dreaming of fishes dancing in my head.

The seaweed’s waltz, quite a funny sight,
Tangled in laughter, it twirls in delight.
Lobsters in bow ties, so dapper and neat,
Serving up jokes with their crustacean beat.

The crabs hold meetings by the shore,
Debating which tourists they should implore.
With pinch of humor, they scutter away,
While I chuckle at their silly ballet.

As I drift off to slumber so sweet,
The lullabies echo, my dreams find their feet.
Each wave a whisper, each splash a tease,
In this quirky nocturne, I dance with ease.

Serene Whispers from the Deep

Below the surface, the fish do conspire,
In fin-flapping laughter, their voices aspire.
A turtle's slow dance, remarkably sly,
With bubbles for jokes, how they make me cry!

The octopus juggles its treasures with glee,
Holding sea rocks as if they were free,
While starfish applaud with their five-pointed claps,
From sandy stages, they guffaw and tap.

Whispers of the deep, so calm yet so bright,
A world of mischief hidden from sight.
The currents swirl with a playful breeze,
Telling tales of tricksters beneath the seas.

As I float above, with laughter I dive,
Imagining how they feel so alive.
In this serene world, humor hides deep,
Where the sea's gentle whispers cradle my sleep.

The Alchemy of Sea and Sky

The ocean laughed at the sky,
As clouds wore a moody frown.
Seagulls danced like they were high,
While crabs tried to wear a crown.

Waves whispered jokes to the shore,
Tickling toes with a frothy cheer.
The sun tossed forth a golden score,
While kites dipped low, full of cheer.

Starfish played cards on the sand,
Winning bets with their lucky fins.
Mermaids cheered, things were unplanned,
Who knew such mischief would begin?

Seashells giggled, a secret tune,
As flip-flops danced with a happy flop.
Underneath this wide afternoon,
The world spun fast, a playful bop.

Twilight's Herald from the Ocean's Mouth

The sunset blushed, a cheeky tease,
As dolphins cracked jokes in a splash.
Stars started winking through the trees,
While crabs plotted their midnight dash.

Bubbles rose with a goofy pop,
As fish held a bubbling soirée.
The laughter echoed, wouldn't stop,
With jesters weaving through the spray.

Shells shed their pearls, a grand affair,
And seagulls squawked their feathered glee.
With every wave and every glare,
Current jokes flowed, wild and free.

The breezy jesters filled the night,
As sandcastles wore funny hats.
From sunrise's giggle to moonlight,
The ocean hums, a world of spats.

Scented Hints of the Briny Abyss

Whiffs of mischief rode the swell,
As barnacles threw a wild ball.
An octopus spun a tall tale,
While jellyfish pulled off a crawl.

The tide brought gossip from afar,
With glimmers flashing silly pranks.
Each wave a secret, every star,
Shared grins with bubbles, fun-filled tanks.

Seashells dropped hints of the day,
With sandy whispers all around.
Crabs scuttled off in bright dismay,
Chasing down waves that twirled unbound.

The breeze chuckled, a gleeful friend,
While fish formed bands with rhythmic splashes.
In the briny realm, fun won’t end,
As laughter roars in playful clashes.

Nautical Serenade in the Evening Air

The flute of the sea, a sweet façade,
As boats performed a silly dance.
Anchors swayed, oh, what a charade,
While sailors crafted their romance.

Each wave a verse in this grand tune,
As gulls serenaded the moonlight.
Paddles clapped in a joyful swoon,
Under stars that twinkled so bright.

Harbors hummed a witty refrain,
With fishermen debating their catch.
The winds played tricks, not quite the same,
As laughter surged, hard to match.

As night wore on, the fun did grow,
With lanterns glowing, spirits lifted.
The sea's own magic stole the show,
In nautical dreams, all souls drifted.

Beneath a Canopy of Sea Mist

Beneath the mists where seagulls squawk,
A crab in pajamas does a little walk.
The jellyfish dance in that wet, wild trance,
While starfish take turns at a conga romance.

A fisherman sneezes, his catch slips away,
He swears it's the tide that led him astray.
But the fish, they're just laughing, a fin-dazzled crew,
Sipping kelp cocktails, in a seaweed stew.

An octopus waves with a comical grin,
Telling tales of the whirlpools — where do I begin?
A clam steals the show, with a pearl in its sight,
Guess who’s ready for the underwater night?

The dolphins chase waves, like kids in the sun,
Racing each other—oh, isn’t this fun?
While the tide rolls in, with a whoosh and a splash,
Beneath this canopy, we'll make quite the crash!

Rhapsody of the Coastal Zephyr

A breeze whirls in, and the kites take flight,
They twist and they twirl in a wonderful sight.
A picnic goes wild with a gusty surprise,
As sandwiches leap up to the laugh of the skies.

Beach balls go bouncing, oh, what a scene,
While the seagulls debate who gets the ice cream.
One bird tries to swoop but bumps into a hat,
He struts off in style, remains none the fat.

Tide pools are jiving, with fish on the scene,
They wiggle and giggle in waters once serene.
A crab pulls a trick, dons a flip-flop shoe,
While a shoal of small minnows plans a debut.

The sunset sparks laughter, colors run wild,
As kids splash about, the sea's favored child.
Under this rhapsody, we dance on the shore,
Finding joy in the chaos, forever wanting more!

Breaths of the Deep Blue

The ocean's a mime with its giggles and sighs,
Puffing up pufferfish, with balloon-like eyes.
A dolphin names Timmy plays tag with a shoe,
As crabs stand in line for a dance at the zoo.

The waves toss in laughter, they bubble and foam,
Shells are the treasures we find when we roam.
A clam gives a wink, says, 'You're all just too mainstream,'
While starfish roll over, caught up in a dream.

Lobsters have parties with hats on their claws,
While fish trade their secrets, all just because.
A quirky parade moves along the wet sand,
With beach attire awkward, it's perfectly planned.

The deep blue's a canvas, art made with glee,
Where each splash and each wave sings in harmony.
Dancing with sea creatures and bubbles that pop,
Here laughter floats up, and never will stop!

A Farewell to the Glistening Horizon

The horizon waves bye, with a wink and a grin,
As sun-hats go flying, amid all the din.
Umbrellas, like jellyfish, ride off in delight,
They're taking the beach chairs to a dance through the night.

Children chase shadows, flip-flops on the run,
While waves rattle secrets of mischief and fun.
A mermaid peeks out, with a wink and a swish,
Says, 'Catch me if you can!' with a fishy little wish.

Sandcastles stand tall, but they wobble with glee,
As a crab bolts through, pretending to flee.
The tide comes to tickle, as laughter breaks loose,
Building dreams in the grains, our minds cut them loose.

Farewell, dear horizon, till next time we meet,
With sand in our toes, and the world at our feet.
We'll laugh with the swells, till the shadows grow long,
In this raucous sea symphony, we all belong!

A Romantic Prelude of the High Tide

The seagulls squawk their silly song,
As beachball warriors battle along.
With ice cream cones that slide and drip,
One wrong move, it's a tasty trip!

In flip-flops, we dance on the shore,
Mixing laughter with ocean's roar.
A crab scuttles by with a shake of its claw,
Judging our moves with a look of 'maw!'

Sunburnt noses, oh what a sight,
Trying to dodge the waves with delight.
But each splash brings squeals and grins,
As we wrestle with these salty whims!

Our picnic blankets gracefully slide,
As we chase after chips that tried to hide.
With each wave's crash, our worries fade,
In this prelude where fun is made!

Sundown Whispers from the Ocean's Heart

The sun dips low, but our jokes stay high,
As twilight paints a silly sky.
We try to catch fireflies for a show,
But they just laugh and take flight—oh no!

With sandy toes, we chase the night,
Spotting stars while feeling light.
The tide rolls in with a frothy cheer,
Playing tag with whispers, oh so near!

The moon winks down, a cheeky chap,
While we lay back, taking a nap.
A crab photobombs our dreamy spree,
We giggle as it scuttles away with glee!

As shadows dance with a twinkly tune,
We crown ourselves rulers of the dune.
With laughter ringing far and wide,
We end the night, our joy can't hide!

Rhythms of the Deep Blue Expanse

Waves that waltz in a giggling parade,
While fish below join in the charade.
A dolphin dons a hat made of foam,
We clap and cheer for our sea-going gnome!

With a splash and a dive, he shows us his move,
A flip and a swirl, he's got all the groove.
We try to mimic his gliding flair,
But end up flopping, gasping for air!

The salty air tickles our nose,
As we spot a jellyfish striking a pose.
With a wink and a jig, it twirls in delight,
And we laugh till we ache under the starlight.

In the depths where the treasure maps start,
With laughter intertwined, we share our heart.
The ocean’s rhythm, a comedic tune,
Echoing softly under the watchful moon!

Traces of a Mariner's Tale

In a boat made of hopes and some old wood,
We sail on dreams seeking all things good.
With fishing lines made of jokes and strings,
We reel in laughs as the seagull sings!

The captain's hat sits crooked and torn,
As we battle the breeze just after dawn.
An octopus joins for a game of charades,
Making faces that crack us in spades!

Our compass spins, lost in our glee,
While mermaids giggle, swimming free.
We spill our snacks upon the floor,
Sharing tales of 'what's behind that door?'

Every wave a punchline, every splash a cheer,
We write our own saga with no hint of fear.
For in this adventure, a crew full of jest,
We've found the treasure—the laughter, the best!

Flavors of Freedom in Every Gust

The wind comes in with a snicker,
Tickling noses, oh what a kicker!
It whispered secrets, oh how it teased,
With each puff, our worries eased.

A shrimp flew by, wearing shades of blue,
Said, "Hey there, want to be a fish too?"
I laughed so hard, nearly fell in,
Who knew seafood had such a grin?

The seagulls squawk in a chorus of glee,
Dancing in rhythm, wild and free.
They’ve got the moves, like they own the show,
Making me wonder if I should join in the flow.

With every gust, comes a quirky smell,
Mix of sunscreen and seaweed as well.
A flavor explosion, unexpected and bright,
Who knew fresh air could taste so right?

The Wild Symphony of Ocean Winds

Listen close, the wind will play,
A melody that steals the day.
It frolics through the beach with style,
Causing beach balls to bounce like a child.

The kites are soaring, what a sight!
Like jellyfish in an airborne fight.
Each gust a laugh, a playful tease,
Whipping up fun with effortless ease.

The sandcastles are wobbling, looking quite grand,
Until the keen wind gives a gentle hand.
They tumble and topple, a sandy retreat,
As the shore takes a stroll on little hairy feet.

Oh, the splashes from waves join the fun,
A riotous dance, a race that can’t be outrun.
Nature’s comedy show, happening live,
With every puff, our spirits dive!

Tide-Pool Reflections and Airy Echoes

In a tide pool, life's wrapped in glee,
Starfish grinning, crabs waving at me.
They're plotting world domination, I swear,
As I watch them shuffle without a care.

The wind chimes in with a breezy joke,
Tickling the seaweed, oh how it spoke!
"Why did the fish blush?" it spun with flair,
"Because it saw the ocean's bottom bare!"

Shimmering reflections dance on the waves,
Giggling at shadows, oh how it raves!
The clams are clamoring in chorus, it's true,
"Can we join the band? We can skewer a tune!"

With each gust that tickles and shakes,
Comes laughter aplenty, oh what a mix!
The sea is a stage, the sand is a seat,
A comedy act, oh isn't it sweet?

Seabound Fantasies on the Currents

The boat bobbles, a dance with the tide,
As if it knows secrets we all should hide.
The wind whispers tales of uncharted lands,
Where sea monsters roast marshmallows on sands.

Seagulls gossip about pirate schemes,
While dolphins flip, living out dreams.
They wink at the boat, a cheeky delight,
As if to say, “Join the fun in flight!”

The sunscreen brigade is hard at work,
Slathering on lotions with a quirky smirk.
“Don’t forget my back!” I call out with cheer,
As the wind shouts back, “You missed a spot, dear!”

The tide brings along a whimsical scent,
Of fishy adventures and sun’s advent.
In this watery wonder, joy flows like frills,
With laughter and fun, we're chasing the thrills!

Murmurs from the Edge of Existence

Waves giggle as they splash in play,
A seagull stole my lunch today.
Sandcastles wobble, laugh and fall,
"Who built this?" we ask the seagull's call.

Jellyfish dance with graceful flops,
I trip and stumble, then it stops.
A crab waves back with a sideways strut,
Whiskers twitch in a sandy rut.

Shells whisper tales of days gone by,
While sunburns risk a lobster’s fry.
Oh, the ocean's wild and wacky jest,
Who knew a wave would know me best?

Laughing tides roll on with glee,
A surfboard took my dignity!
With every splash, a comic scene,
Embraced by ocean, oh so keen!

Driftwood Memories and Airborne Secrets

Drifting logs with faces grim,
Moaning secrets on a whim.
Sand fleas dance like they're on fire,
What's on the menu? Crabs—dinner's dire.

Ocean mist tickles my nose,
As flip-flops gather seaweed woes.
A gull's squawk beats our laughter loud,
As bikini fails leave us cowed.

Seashells hold gossip of the sea,
Our beach day fails—oh dearie me!
With sunscreen smeared from head to toe,
I look like I'm ready for a snowshow!

The tides retreat with a playful shove,
Bringing footprints, even a love.
Memories drift like ships at bay,
Crazy fun, until it's time to pay!

Echoes of the Nautical Depths

A fishy tale from down below,
Where sharks wear hats and lobsters glow.
Echoes bounce through watery halls,
Worms boasts of their intricate squalls.

A mermaid laughs at lousy lines,
While crustaceans plot their dining designs.
Octopus jokes and undersea pranks,
Leave jellyfish rolling in giggles and thanks.

Sunken ships hold buried dreams,
While barnacles form team-building schemes.
Pirates arguing about their loot,
Wishing for eggs, “No more rotten fruit!”

With every splash that moonbeams reflect,
The ocean sings; it’s quite the spectacle!
We paddle along to a chorus of cheer,
Waving goodbye to all that's queer!

Whispered Journeys on the Horizon

Winds of whimsy beguile the day,
As I surf on a cloud, then sway.
The sun-god chuckles, tickling my back,
Clouds toss their popcorn— it's a snack attack!

With boat shoes on, we trip and slide,
Finding treasure and a jellyfish ride.
A dolphin leaps with a splashy grin,
"Catch me if you can!"—the fun begins.

Whispers of fun travel like smoke,
While friends fall over in surfboards' choke.
Kites soar high, a colorful dance,
Even the sea turtles join the chance!

At dusk, we gather 'round the fire's glow,
Telling tales of the sea's wild show.
With laughter and guffaws to light the night,
Life's a beach, what a funny sight!

Gossamer Waves and Wind

The gulls squawk tales of lost fries,
As waves wink in their disguise.
Sandcastles crumble like old bread,
Who knew the tides liked to spread?

Flip-flops flinging, what a sight,
A lost game of tag with the light.
Seagulls plotting a theft of shells,
While kids chase dreams, no need for bells.

Kites soaring high, pretending to dive,
The ocean’s giggles keep us alive.
Crabs in tuxedos dance in a line,
Who knew beach days could be so fine?

Sunburnt noses, laughter's loud,
Finding treasures in a watery shroud.
With every splash, we join the spree,
At the world's best comedy, the sea.

Driftwood Secrets in the Zephyr

Driftwood whispers, tales untold,
Of pirates who were a little too bold.
A half-eaten sandwich, rescued by fate,
Turns out it's a mermaid’s dinner plate!

The breeze plays tricks, a hair-raising game,
With hats that take off, never the same.
Sandy dogs prance, chasing their tails,
While surfers are off reading sea-mail fails.

Crabs hold court in their sandy towns,
Debating the best way to wear crowns.
Wind plays a joke, wraps us in sea,
Laughing with joy as we trip and flee.

A driftwood throne, where seashells are kings,
Celebrating life’s little funny flings.
We dance in the surf, high on our glee,
As nature's wet sketch brings forth our spree.

Aroma of the Coastal Dawn

Morning smells of bacon and sea,
Pancakes flop like fish, oh me!
Waves laugh lightly at the sun’s bright grin,
As sleepy fish wade out on a whim.

The surfboard's waiting, a taco delight,
But first, can I conquer this chocolate bite?
Coffee in hand, it spills like a wave,
A perfect start to a day we crave.

Birds in the air, trying to prank,
Taking bets on who'll dunk in the tank.
Laughter rises with the morning light,
As sunhats sail off in a ridiculous flight.

With every sunrise, silliness grows,
We paddle through life in our flip-flop clothes.
At the dawn of the day, come join the fun,
Where even the ocean says “Oh, what a pun!”

The Serenity of Salty Skies

Clouds of cotton-candy memories drift,
Sea foam tickles toes, oh what a gift!
Tidal waves breaking with comical flair,
A noseful of laughs floats free in the air.

Mussels whisper secrets of seaweed lore,
While snorkels bob underneath the shore.
Kids chase sunlight, shouting with glee,
As sandcastles topple with waves of esprit.

Seashells in hand, we barter for laughs,
Trading our worries for the ocean's graphs.
The lighthouse winks at the goofy tide,
In the salty embrace, come take a ride.

With every tide, silliness blooms wide,
The sky wraps us in its playful pride.
So let's roll in the surf, with giggles galore,
At the beach of humor, forever we score!

A Symphony of Tides and Wind

The seagulls squawk with glee,
As fish throw pranks below the sea.
A crab does a jig on the sand,
Not sure if he's in a band!

Waves crash and tumble to a tune,
While surfers dance under the moon.
A picnic's set, but ants parade,
Stealing snacks without a trade!

A sandcastle rises, then a flop,
As playful tides won't let it stop.
The sunbeams wink, plans in the air,
One forgotten flip-flop—beware!

So let's laugh loud, share silly tales,
Of one-legged crabs and curious snails.
In this salty realm, joy finds its way,
As we unwind, laugh, and play!

The Call of the Brackish Waters

Oh, the fish here have such flair,
Wearing goggle-style sunglasses, they stare.
A dolphin’s doing tricks galore,
While boaters shout, “Just one more!”

Pelicans dive with quite the style,
Stealing snacks—oh, have a smile!
A sea turtle slows for a snack,
With a wink and a lazy smack!

Jellyfish dance in the splashing foam,
Inviting us to join their home.
But careful now, they sting a bit,
Just wave back but don’t commit!

Here in this chaos, laughter rings,
Where even the seaweed dances with flings.
Let’s toast the tides, both weird and wacky,
With a splash, a giggle, life’s never tacky!

Ocean-Misted Dreams at Twilight

At dusk the beach becomes a show,
Where crabs moonwalk, stealing the glow.
A starfish steals the limelight, too,
Waving arms like, “Look at me, boo!”

The waves blush pink from the setting sun,
Singing a tune, we all join in fun.
A slight breeze tickles, causing a cheer,
As wind whispers secrets for all to hear.

A bottle’s washed up with a note,
“Need a ride? I’ll float!” the message wrote.
But gulls grab it first, play catch and bite,
What a raucous scene in twilight's light!

Here dreams bob like corks on the tide,
With each wave, joy is our guide.
So laugh with the sea, and let hearts sway,
In this whimsical world, forever play!

Unraveled Threads of Mariner's Sigh

The sailor grumbles, his hat’s gone askew,
As a rogue wave tosses his breakfast stew.
Fish leap high, like they’re on a spree,
While he just wants some peace with his tea!

The winds conspire, tickling his beard,
While a gull swoops down, his lunch disappeared.
“Don’t eat my fries!” he shouts with glee,
But the bird just laughs, “I’m still hungry!”

Nets are tangled, boats weave a dance,
Caught in laughs, they miss their chance.
A dolphin spins, the crew’s in a spin,
Mocking their woes with a cheeky grin!

Under the stars, they blow off some steam,
Life’s too short, so let’s guffaw and dream.
With every guff, our troubles will fade,
Sailing through life’s mishaps—unafraid!

Ebbing Thoughts of the Rolling Sea

Waves crash with a giggle, oh so clear,
Tickling toes, providing cheer.
Seagulls swoop with a silly shout,
Plucking snacks from folks about.

Sunburned noses and hats askew,
Fried clam smells waft, quite askew.
Sandcastles teeter, then they fall,
Laughter echoes, we have a ball.

Fishes whisper jokes below,
As tide and time play to and fro.
A crab does a jig, quite in his zone,
Clapping claws, the sea's own bone.

Ebbing thoughts, like surf retreat,
Chasing laughter, oh so sweet.
With every crest, the fun renews,
In this salty world, we can't lose.

Shimmering Hues on the Wind

Kites dance up in the bright blue sky,
Tangled in laughter as they fly high.
Children chase dreams in neon hues,
While sticky fingers munch on snooze.

Shells reflect giggles, soft and bright,
Sunshine and silliness in full sight.
The breeze carries snippets of delight,
As flip-flops flounder in playful flight.

Old whispers of jelly, oh so sweet,
Messy ice cream drips on our feet.
With every gust, a chuckle starts,
Binding joy in our silly hearts.

Waves tug at ankles, laughter ignites,
Tiny crabs boogie, oh what sights!
In this realm of shimmer and grin,
Just breathe in fun, let joy begin.

Conch Shell Songs from the Shore

Conch shells sing with voices of glee,
Harmonizing with the melody of the sea.
Waves join in, with a playful roar,
Creating symphonies on the sandy floor.

Crabs engage in a dance-off bold,
Their tiny steps, a sight to behold.
As dolphins whistle, prancing along,
The ocean hums a joyful song.

Sandcastles crumble with a chuckle loud,
As tourists gather, quite a crowd.
Each grain of sand trapped in a giggle,
Tide-tide tickles, then takes a wiggle.

Breezes carry our laughter away,
In this seaside haven, we play.
Every conch, a tale to tell,
Echoing joy from shore to shell.

Mapping Dreams in the Salty Summer

Beneath the sun, we ride the tide,
With whimsical maps where we abide.
Flip-flops squeak, a rhythmic tune,
As we chase shadows and fade by noon.

Popsicles drip down fingers to the sand,
Sticky treasures crafted by hand.
Dreams float by like ships on the way,
Charting laughter’s course, come what may.

Each splash and roar, a daring quest,
Who can hold onto the sand’s jest?
Seashells whisper, secrets unfold,
Picture-perfect tales of laughter to hold.

Summer nights wrapped in ocean’s embrace,
With stars above adding to the grace.
In salty air, hearts start to roam,
Mapping dreams, we’re never alone.

Whispers of the Tidal Air

The gulls are laughing, what a sight,
As they steal my sandwich, oh what a fright!
Waves crash and tumble, dancing about,
While I chase my hat that the wind's blown out.

Seagulls gossip, they squawk and they cheer,
I wave my arms, but they just won't hear.
Shells are the treasure, yet where are the gems?
Just bits of old plastic and fishermen's hems.

Beach balls are bouncing like they have a plan,
They land on strangers—what a madman!
Chasing down shadows, we laugh in dismay,
The tide pulls us closer, then sweeps us away.

With sand in my shoes and a grin on my face,
I'm a merry clown, fit for this place.
The ocean is hosting a whimsical show,
And I can't help it—time to let go!

A Symphony of Ocean Kisses

The waves compose music, a merry tune,
Each splash and each crash, a splashy cartoon.
Seashells rolling like marbles on sand,
While I build a castle, it's crooked but grand!

The wind is a prankster, it tugs at my hat,
I jump and I giggle, oh, look at that!
A crab in my bucket, he's thinking he's sly,
But he can't escape—oh, me oh my!

Children are squealing, running amok,
With ice cream in hand, they've run out of luck.
I slip on a puddle, a splash and a yelp,
This beach party's wild and full of itself!

Caught in the laughter, the waves sing along,
This coastline's a stage for our wobbly throng.
With the sun in our eyes and the sand beneath,
We dance to the rhythm, it's hard to believe!

The Breath of Briny Dreams

Watching the fisher's parade through the mist,
With nets full of goodies, oh sweet twist!
They trip on their lines, and fish start to fly,
While I'm just here wondering why I can't try.

The cocktail of seaweed is way over-hyped,
Yet crabs seem to dance, oh, they're so well-typed!
"Why don't you come out?" I say with a grin,
But crabs just retreat with a wave of their fin.

A dolphin pokes out and gives me a wink,
I swear he's a prankster, not just what you think.
He splashes and giggles, then dives out of sight,
Leaving me chuckling as day turns to night.

The horizon is painted in hues of delight,
With laughter as bubbles ascend to great height.
The sea whispers secrets, both silly and grand,
As I dream on the shore, with my love by hand.

Echoes of the Sea's Embrace

The ocean calls out with a bubbly cheer,
"Wear your goggles, my friend, don't you fear!"
With sea foam and laughter, we tumble and spin,
The waves are a chorus; let's all dive in!

I spot a mermaid, or is it a sock?
With all of this water, who gives it a stop?
The fish gossip loudly, all in a school,
While I shout to a turtle, "Hey, what's the rule?"

Sandcastle kingdoms rise, but they tumble at dusk,
The tide is a thief, leaving nothing but musk.
We chase all the shells, with love in the chase,
And giggle at jellyfish dancing with grace.

Breezy shenanigans, and giggles in waves,
The ocean's our playground, where frolic behaves.
With each splash and roar, we lose track of time,
In the arms of the sea, it's all pure good rhyme!

When Tides Whisper Love

When the waves flirt with the land,
Seagulls sing a silly band.
I chase crabs across the sand,
While jellyfish wave, unplanned.

Shells are hiding, what a sight,
One just winked, oh what a fright!
The hermit crabs play dress-up fun,
Stealing shells like they just won.

The beach ball rolls, a sandy thief,
I dive in, but butt, no relief!
Giggles echo, splashes fly,
Sea foam tickles as I cry.

When the tide pulls back to play,
I'll build a castle, hip-hip-hooray!
Adventure waits with each new wave,
A laugh, a splash, my heart, it braves.

Drifted Thoughts of a Shoreline Heart

A starfish danced, it stole my heart,
As crabs perform their own fine art.
Finicky fish swim by with glee,
A silly sight—oh, look at me!

The tides gossip, oh what a crew,
With sandy secrets, just for two.
Laughs collide in a watery chat,
While I lose my flip-flop to a cat.

Waves roll in with a cheerful tease,
Whispers tickle through the trees.
I spot a dolphin, grinning wide,
Can it be? I've found my tide!

A beach party forms with joyful cheer,
Laughter rings, I cannot steer.
With sunscreen smeared upon my nose,
I dance with waves; nobody knows!

Caressing Winds and Ocean Hues

The wind tickles my cheek with flair,
While kites above do float and dare.
A seagull swoops, insists on fries,
I can’t help but laugh at its slight size.

With buckets filled, we build and play,
Sandcastles high, like dreams at bay.
But tidal waves love a surprise,
And down they crash, oh how it flies!

I spot a crab in disco mode,
Shaking claws down the sandy road.
The seaweed sways, a funky twist,
A dance-off soon, who can resist?

Among the waves, with cheer, we rest,
Covered in laughter, we feel so blessed.
Shells in pockets, and hearts in tow,
The shore’s our stage, enjoy the show!

Mists of the Marine World

In the fog, a mermaid grins wide,
With fishy friends, they take a ride.
My sunglasses fogged, can't see a thing,
But laughter bubbles, oh what joy it brings!

The tide pulls back, a goofy prank,
My toes are wet, wherever I sank.
Octopus chuckles, a tentacled clown,
Juggling shells while I'm just drowned.

The breeze plays tricks on my wild hair,
A tumbleweed floats without a care.
As I dance with prawns, oh life’s a blast,
The ocean's laughter is unsurpassed.

With misty air and giggles bright,
The day rolls on, from morn till night.
Here at the shore, where fun's our quest,
I'll chase the waves, it's simply the best!

Spirited Winds of the Faraway

The wind's a playful fellow, you see,
Tickling the waves, doing a jig with glee.
Seagulls laugh as they swoop and dive,
While the sand tickles toes, oh, how they thrive!

A crab, quite the dancer, moves to the beat,
Waving his claws, he feels quite the feat.
But watch your sandwich, or it'll be gone!
The wind whispers jokes, and the waves just yawn!

With shells as their instruments, they make quite the show,
As the ocean's own band starts to ebb and flow.
Flip-flops go flying, what a glorious sight,
As the sun paints the sky, turning day into night!

So join in the laughter, let your worries fly,
For the spirited winds are here to satisfy.
Catch a wave of joy, let your spirit soar high,
In this whimsical world where the wild things lie!

Seafoam Dreams and Wandering Spirits

A wave rolls in with a cheeky grin,
Spraying saltwater for a playful spin.
The beach ball's off-bouncing, oh what a chase!
As we stumble and tumble, we can’t keep pace!

Funky flip-flops and dodgy hats,
The ocean’s a fountain for silly sprats.
Seashells gossip as they overhear,
While a sunburned tourist sips his ice-cold beer!

And look, there’s a dolphin, performing a trick,
Belly-flopping into the waves, oh so quick!
The sea foam giggles, tickling our toes,
As the tide plays its tricks, anything goes!

So raise your voice to the charming sea,
Dance with the waves, and just be free.
In this realm of quirkiness, join the display,
Where dreams sprinkle down like grains of hay!

The Breath of the Shoreline

The shoreline whispers with a laugh and a roar,
As waves make their entrance, crashing the shore.
Tide pools are playgrounds for tiny lime fish,
Who bubble and wiggle like they're granted a wish!

Old sandals lie scattered, a museum of woe,
As seagulls have meetings, high up in a row.
"Who stole my fries?" one squawks with a huff,
While the wind just chuckles, 'The breeze is quite stuffed!'

So we gather our treasures, the driftwood and shells,
As the sea's playful spirit with humor compels.
And when we get doused by a wave's sneaky prank,
We laugh and we shriek, saying, "We've been blanked!"

With a heart full of giggles, let's stake our claim,
On this magical beach where we dance without shame.
As the sun bids farewell, in the evening's cool light,
We'll treasure these moments, our spirits take flight!

Windswept Memories in Ebb and Flow

The wind brings a tale or a dance full of cheer,
As it twirls through the grass, or whispers so near.
With kites soaring high, like dreams in the air,
We laugh with the clouds, free and debonair!

Oh, the mishaps we cherish, like flipping canoe,
When a wave sneaks up, and our snacks are askew.
"Not my sandwich!" we yell, but the tide simply grins,
As it flips and it flops, drenching all it spins!

With sand between toes and a hat blown away,
The seagulls are laughing, "Join in on the play!"
A crab plays the maracas, what a funny scene,
As the sea strums its lute, so wild and serene!

So let your spirit soar, let the memories stay,
In this world of wonder where silliness plays.
The windswept adventures await on the shore,
With whispers of laughter and stories galore!

A Cascade of Dreams upon the Wind

Seagulls squawk, they steal my fries,
I chase them down, oh what a surprise!
The sand sticks tight to my flip-flop sole,
I trip and fall, but still, I roll.

The waves giggle, they're teasing me,
I splash back hard, oh what glee!
A crab scuttles by, doing a dance,
I join in too, in my summer pants.

A beach ball pops, oh what a sound,
Drifting laughter all around.
Umbrellas flip like hats in a storm,
Who knew chaos could be so warm?

In the distance, a kite takes flight,
I wave at it—what a silly sight!
Today’s adventure is hilariously wild,
Like a sunburned adult acting like a child!

Evening's Embrace at Water's Edge

The tide rolls in, with a frothy slosh,
I dip my toes, feel the cool swash.
My ice cream drips, a sticky affair,
A race with seagulls? I’m unaware!

Shells decorate the shore like jewels,
I pick one up, it’s the queen of fools!
A wave crashes, fills my shoes with foam,
Goodbye dry feet, welcome to wet-comb!

Kids bounce by, with laughter bright,
Building castles, what a sight!
Then they tumble, heads first in sand,
Their giggles echo—it's unplanned!

As the sun dips low and colors explode,
I brace for a sunset, on this sandy road.
But a spray of water catches my face,
Oh well, I’m just embracing the misplaced grace!

The Softness of Waves in Glistening Light

Waves whisper secrets, soft as a sigh,
I can’t resist, I must give it a try!
With each gentle roll, they pull at my toes,
A funny little dance, I must strike a pose!

In the sun’s glow, my reflection does gleam,
Yet my hat flies off—oh, not in my dream!
Chasing it down, much to my dismay,
But laughter erupts, I can’t walk away!

Sandcastles crumble, a fate unforeseen,
I declare war with my friend, in this scene!
Our buckets collide, with a splash and a cheer,
Who knew the beach could bring so much gear?

With dusk approaching, the day starts to fade,
I ponder my choices, can I trade?
Falling on sand? It’s not such a woe,
With a sprinkle of sunshine, I’m ready to go!

Celestial Echoes from the Shoreline

Stars peek through as daylight slips,
A beach bonfire, and marshmallow dips.
Food flies around—oops, there goes the s'more,
Caught by a friend, who lets out a roar!

The moonlight dances on waves that sway,
And I dance too—just a little cliché.
With wobbly feet, I trip on my way,
Laughter erupts, brightening the gray.

Tide pools glitter as we gawk and stare,
What's that slimy thing? A creature quite rare?
We poke and prod, only to find,
It's our lost sandwich—oh, never mind!

In the night's embrace, we share silly tales,
Of epic fails and crosswind gales.
As the waves recede, so do our fears,
For humor lives always, throughout the years!

Curls of Seafoam in the Air

The sea's a jester, wild and bright,
It tosses bubbles in delight.
I duck and weave, what a surprise,
A foam-filled prank right before my eyes.

Waves take turns to splash my face,
The surf's a giggle; oh, what a race!
Seaweed's tangled, it pulls my shoe,
Curls of laughter, who knew it'd do?

A dolphin leaps, like it's a show,
Judging my dance, oh no, oh no!
Each splash a chuckle, the tide's good cheer,
I clap my hands, the fish all leer.

In this playful sea, I lose my way,
Each gust a tease, come out and play!
With seafoam giggles, I take my stance,
A comedy sketch in the ocean's dance.

Moments Caught in Ocean’s Caress

A crab with swagger walks the line,
Claws raised high, thinks it’s divine.
I laugh and trip on shifting sand,
As foam folks giggle, oh what a band!

The tide retreats, just for a while,
Shells whisper secrets, yet still smile.
With a wink and nod, they gather near,
As waves crash forth with a hearty cheer.

A seagull swoops low for my snack,
I swat it away, then it comes back.
In moments caught, we share the fun,
Beneath the sun, life’s just begun!

Each splash and plop, a joke well-told,
The ocean's antics never get old.
With sand in my shoes, I wave goodbye,
To every chuckle beneath the sky.

Whims of the Shoreline Spirit

A beach ball bounces, oh so bright,
It rolls away, much to my fright.
Chasing after, I trip on a shell,
The shoreline giggles, all is well.

Kites dance high, in the wind's embrace,
Crashing waves join in the race.
I shout at the clouds, in playful jest,
As the tide teases, I feel so blessed.

Footprints joke, they wander in line,
Climbing dunes, feeling fine.
I toss a stick, it floats away,
The shoreline spirit, here to play!

With laughter echoing, the sun dips low,
The day winds down with a fun-filled glow.
In every ripple, a giggly tune,
The beach my stage, beneath the moon.

A Dance Amongst the Dunes

Sand dunes shimmy, a lively sight,
I twirl in joy, just pure delight.
The wind spins tales, whispers in glee,
As laughter dances, wild and free.

With sun hats flapping, we take our stand,
The shifting sands, a playful band.
Each tumble and roll, a funny spree,
The dunes play tricks, just wait and see!

Seashells clink like chimes on high,
Together we laugh, oh my, oh my!
A tumbleweed joins the cheerful flow,
In this sandy ball, let's steal the show!

As twilight falls, the stars peek through,
Whispers of fun hang in the dew.
With every giggle, we sway and lean,
In this dance of dunes, a scene serene.

Breezes that Taste of Adventure

A wandering seagull stole my hat,
With a squawk and a flap, imagine that!
Left my head bare, a sun-bright mess,
Chasing that bird was pure silliness.

The ocean's charm in each playful wave,
Tickled my toes, like a bubbly grave.
With friends laughing loud, we splashed around,
Life’s an amusement park, joy unbound.

Riding inflatable ducks, what a sight!
We floated in circles, oh what a plight.
The sunbeams winked, the laughter grew,
At least the ducks knew just what to do!

As the tide pulled back, they'd hoot and holler,
A raucous crew with grit and valor.
Adventure awaits in every puff,
And when you stumble? Just laugh it off!

Hidden Stories in the Sea's Aroma

A fishy tale whispers from the shore,
Of treasures lost and the ocean's lore.
I found a shoe that once was grand,
It must've danced on dreamy sand.

A crab went by in his tiny car,
Honking loudly, what a bizarre!
I offered him chips, and off he sped,
Mumbling crumbs and nodding his head.

Seagulls gossip like old folks do,
"Did you hear about the fish that flew?"
Bubbles giggle as the waves swirl wide,
While barnacles share their secrets inside.

Each scent that wafts tells stories untold,
Of shipwrecked hearts and brave souls bold.
So next time you sniff the ocean's scent,
Remember its laughter in every bent!

The Dance of Waves and Time

The waves are dancers with no shy feet,
Twisting and twirling to a breezy beat.
With each splash, they throw a party,
Wave-hopping fellows acting quite hearty.

Shells are the claps in this watery show,
Applauding the rhythm as they gently glow.
The sun joins in with its golden lace,
A disco ball in this aqua space.

Oh, and here comes a flip-flop parade,
Swaying side to side, never afraid.
They trip and they flip, creating a fuss,
"Who knew a footwear would cause such a bus?"

As night falls down with a glint and a shine,
The waves still dance; oh, how they entwine!
With laughter echoing from sea to shore,
It's a party we'll remember forevermore!

Salty Breezes and Starlit Skies

Under starlights that whisper and twinkle,
The salty air made our toes all crinkle.
We built a sandcastle taller than me,
Only to have it swept away with glee.

The moon chuckled, a cheeky old chap,
As we giggled and nibbled from our picnic wrap.
A raccoon joined us, bold and slick,
He grabbed my sandwich and did a quick trick!

“Don’t feed the wildlife!” the signs declare,
But who could resist that furry hair?
In the shimmering night, we plotted our schemes,
With sandwiches missing, but bursting with dreams.

So let the breeze carry our stories far,
Of laughter, mishaps, and wishing on stars.
With each salty wink from the twilight sighs,
We dance with the thrill beneath these skies.

www.ingramcontent.com/pod-product-compliance
Lightning Source LLC
Chambersburg PA
CBHW072129070526
44585CB00016B/1595